ROUSSEAU IN 90 MINUTES

Rousseau
IN 90 MINUTES

Paul Strathern

IVAN R. DEE
CHICAGO

ROUSSEAU IN 90 MINUTES. Copyright © 2002 by Paul
Strathern. All rights reserved, including the right to reproduce
this book or portions thereof in any form. For information,
address: Ivan R. Dee, Publisher, 1332 North Halsted Street,
Chicago 60622. Manufactured in the United States of America
and printed on acid-free paper.

Library of Congress Cataloging-in-Publication Data:
Strathern, Paul, 1940–
    Rousseau in 90 minutes / Paul Strathern.
      p. cm.
    Includes bibliographical references and index.
    ISBN 1-56663-437-7 (alk. paper) — ISBN 1-56663-436-9
(pbk. : alk. paper)
    1. Rousseau, Jean-Jacques, 1712–1778.   I. Title: Rousseau
in ninety minutes.   II. Title.
B2137 .S77 2002
194—dc21   2002019500

Contents

ROUSSEAU IN 90 MINUTES

Introduction

Rousseau was a contemporary of such supreme philosophers as Kant and Hume, yet his popular influence far exceeded either. Kant and Hume may have been superior academic philosophers, but the sheer power of Rousseau's ideas was unequaled in his time. Indeed, Rousseau was certainly the most unintellectual of all the great philosophers. Again and again, feeling triumphs over intellectual argument in his works—which are both deeply stirring and deeply inconsistent. It is possible simultaneously to both love and hate Rousseau—for his work as well as for his effect. It was he who encouraged the introduction of both liberty and irrationality into the public domain.

The man and his ideas were one. Rousseau lived out his thought to the very utmost of his being. As a man he was both endearing and impossible. Here was a walking ego, a naked sensibility. For Rousseau, normal everyday life was often a torment—and he often made sure it was for those around him. But Europe was in need of such a figure. By the early years of the eighteenth century, when Rousseau was born, the scientific revolution and the Enlightenment were giving rise to great intellectual advances. Yet at the same time the European sensibility was suffering from a deep malaise. It had become bogged down in the intellectual and emotional restraints of classicism. In the midst of the new progress, many individuals were aware that they were beginning to lose touch with themselves, with who they really were. This was a novel feeling— which would remain part of our sensibility to this day. Rousseau was the first to confront this inarticulate self-awareness. It was he who insisted that we should seek out and experience our "true nature."

Rousseau's Life and Works

Jean-Jacques Rousseau was born on June 28, 1712, at Geneva in Switzerland. He never knew his mother, who died of the effects of childbirth ten days after his arrival. In his own words: "My birth was the first of my misfortunes. . . . I was born almost dying, they had little hope of saving me. I carried the seed of a disorder that the years have reinforced." This was how Rousseau viewed his entry into the world: a drama whose potential "disorder" would prove emotional, psychological, and even physical. From the start, his relationship with those around him was unhealthily intense. His father, a watchmaker who had married "above his social class," was inconsolable at the loss of the woman he had loved since childhood. In Rousseau's words, "He thought he saw her again in me, but could not forget that I had robbed him of her." They would both cry when he spoke of her. "He never kissed me without my being aware of his sighs; in his convulsive hugs a bitter grief was mingled with his caresses." One can all but hear, feel, and smell the closeness and undermining ambivalence.

There appears to have been a streak of impulsive wildness in the family. Rousseau had a brother who was seven years older than him. His father would occasionally beat the brother, and on one occasion Rousseau flung himself between them to save his brother. Rousseau at first describes his brother as a "rascal" but later reveals, "Finally my brother turned so bad that he ran away and disappeared completely."

At this time Geneva was a small Protestant republic surrounded by Catholic states and dependencies. It was geographically isolated from its neighbors by the ice-capped peaks of the Alps and the picturesque waters of Lake Geneva. The city owed its republicanism and independence to the sixteenth-century religious reformer John

Calvin, who had made it a bastion of Protestantism. Its citizens were upright and democratic. Rousseau's father was intensely proud of his native city, describing it to his son in terms of Sparta and ancient Rome. Rousseau's mother had left them a small library of books, and his father would read them with his son after supper. Soon they both became so absorbed in this activity that they would continue into the night, taking turns to read. "We could never stop before the end of the book. Sometimes when my father heard the larks at daybreak, he would be ashamed and exclaim, 'Let's go to bed. I'm more of a child than you.'"

Young Rousseau found himself the center of attention in an almost exclusively female household, with a nurse, an aunt, and occasional admiring relatives. Sitting at his aunt's knee as she embroidered, he would listen to her singing her seemingly endless repertoire of traditional songs. Rousseau was fascinated, acquiring a deep interest and understanding of music at an early age. But the element of undermining ambivalence remained. Years later he would describe himself at this stage as having a "heart at once so proud and so tender [with an] effeminate yet indomitable character . . . vacillating between weakness and courage, self-indulgence and virtue." He saw himself as a "contradiction with myself."

Then, suddenly, everything changed. One day Rousseau's father became involved in a public argument with a local landowner, whom he challenged to a duel. But the landowner contemptuously refused to duel with him because of his lower social origins. Incensed, Rousseau's father drew his sword and struck the landowner on the cheek, drawing blood. Rousseau's father disappeared into exile—in Rousseau's words, "rather than cede a point on which honor and liberty appeared to him compromised"—in fact to avoid a jail sentence. Rousseau's circumstances changed overnight, and he was farmed out to poor relations: a pastor and his sister who lived in a nearby village. While living there he would be subjected to humiliations and beatings by the pastor's sister, which provoked in him a "feeling of violence and injustice." This would have a lasting effect, so that for the rest of his life he could claim that "my blood boils at the spectacle

12

or recital of an unjust act." But these beatings by the parson's sister also induced in him a precocious sexual pleasure which would have an equally lasting effect. "Who could have believed that this punishment received at the age of eight from the hand of a woman of thirty, determined my tastes, my desires, my passions, my very self for the rest of my life." The experience brought to the surface a latent masochism which would characterize his sexuality throughout his life.

At the age of thirteen, Rousseau was apprenticed to an engraver in Geneva. The city may have been a model of righteous democracy, but its Calvinist atmosphere was also puritan and oppressive. This was no place for the likes of Rousseau, who later wrote of himself in these years (indicatively in the third-person present) that "his character derives almost completely from his temperament alone." He was undoubtedly possessed of an intellect, but his reactions were inspired almost entirely by his emotions. "He is what nature has made him—nature has modified him only little." In this self-contradiction lies the essence of Rousseau's thought: even here he is utterly himself. The seeds of the man, his temperament, his entire philosophy lie in this character—which would retain so many of the fervent and unstable qualities of adolescence throughout his life.

Just short of his sixteenth birthday, Rousseau disappeared from Geneva and fled to neighboring Savoy (now part of France, but then under Sardinian control). Here he was soon taken into the household of Madame de Warens, a local landowner who was separated from her aristocratic husband and had converted to Catholicism. The sixteen-year-old Rousseau and the thirty-year-old Mme. de Warens found an immediate rapport. She would convert him to Catholicism, and he would become her pupil. Significantly, he soon began calling her *maman* (mummy). The gauche, stammering apprentice, all but devoid of formal education, who arrived on Mme. de Warens's doorstep was gradually transformed into a presentable young man. Yet this particular ugly duckling would never quite become a swan—beneath the thin social veneer, Rousseau's volatile temperament would continue to be his guiding force.

And he remained very much an innocent.

Not until 1733 did Mme. de Warens finally feel it was her duty to "make a man" of him, seducing her twenty-one-year-old protégé in the little summer house on her estate. For a while Rousseau was installed as a somewhat inept steward to *maman*'s dwindling estate, but later he took on a number of teaching posts at various places in Savoy. The sexual side of his relationship with *maman* would peter out—but she would be a lasting influence on him, and they would remain confidants, corresponding for years to come.

In 1742, at the age of thirty, Rousseau set off to seek fame and fortune in Paris. Despite letters of introduction to a number of minor intellectual figures, Rousseau failed to make an impression, let alone a name for himself. Eventually he was fortunate to be appointed temporary secretary to the French ambassador in Venice, and set off to take up his post. The entire episode was to prove a fiasco. The ambassador, the Comte de Montaigu, was an idle, arrogant aristocrat who looked upon Rousseau as an "impudent upstart" possessed of "all the qualities of a very bad servant." Rousseau, who considered that his

diplomatic status entitled him to be treated almost as an equal, responded with typical temperamental vigor. Surprisingly, this situation
lasted almost twelve months—until the exasper-
ated ambassador finally threatened to throw his
secretary through the window into the canal.

But Rousseau's time in Venice consisted of
more than his involvement in exclusively French
diplomatic incidents. This was the Venice
painted by Canaletto, the "serene republic"
whose sea-trading routes stretched as far as Con-
stantinople and the Levant, a city with a thriving
culture, especially in music. By now Rousseau
had developed his keen ear for music into a full-
fledged talent. He visited the opera frequently
and responded with delight to the tuneful enthu-
siasm and spontaneity of Italian music—which
contrasted sharply with the intricate formality of
French music of the period. He was also enraptured by the more open temperament and bla-
tant sensuality of the Venetian women he
encountered. Most notable of these was a
woman of relaxed virtue called Zulietta. Unfor-
tunately Rousseau still had psychological difficulties where women were concerned. When at

last he found himself alone with the Zulietta, he exclaimed to himself, "Never was such sweet pleasure offered to the heart and senses of a mortal man." But when he found himself unable to rise to the occasion, his eye alighted on her "malformed nipple," whereupon she became transformed in his eyes into "some kind of monster." Zulietta took this in her stride and causally advised him, "Jacko, give up the ladies and study mathematics."

Rousseau also managed to find time for some diplomatic duties. These would have a profound effect. His dealings with the byzantine Venetian authorities opened his eyes to the nature and power of politics. He concluded that "Everything depends entirely upon politics," which meant that "a people is everywhere nothing but what its government makes of it."

Rousseau returned to Paris and once again took up lodgings on the Left Bank "in an ugly room, in an ugly hotel, in an ugly street." This was the Hôtel Saint-Quentin, where one of the staff was an illiterate twenty-two-year-old washerwoman called Thérèse Levasseur. Given the oddities of Rousseau's sexuality, it remains un-

17

clear as to who actually seduced whom—but the result was that Rousseau became her lover. According to Rousseau, he never really loved Thérèse but felt a deep pity for the insults and humiliations she suffered. Yet Thérèse was no innocent victim; in the words of an eyewitness she was "jealous, stupid, gossipy, and a liar." Either way, the two quickly formed a profound and lasting attachment. Thérèse would remain with Rousseau through thick and thin for the rest of his life.

This time Rousseau's efforts to gain recognition were a little more successful. He became acquainted with the intellectual circle known as *Les Philosophes,* the thinkers who were engaged in writing *L'Encyclopédie.* This multi-volume work was intended to promulgate the rational, scientific, and cultural ideas of the Enlightenment. At the time, France was the largest and most powerful nation in Europe, but it remained for the most part rural and backward. The spread of knowledge was seen as the only way of bringing the country into the modern world. France remained under the autocratic *ancien regime,* with the indolent Louis XV and his

18

twenty-thousand-strong court ruling from the gargantuan palace of Versailles, fifteen miles south of Paris. Such free-thinking developments as *L'Encyclopédie* were viewed with deep suspicion by Versailles and the church authorities. Rousseau became a close friend of the philosopher Diderot, the leading light of *L'Encyclopédie* project. Rousseau found the company of *Les Philosophes* intellectually stimulating, and they in turn were intrigued by the passionate temperament and originality of this ambitious provincial. Diderot was particularly impressed by Rousseau's opinions on music, which were backed by considerable knowledge, and he commissioned Rousseau to write a series of articles on music for *L'Encyclopédie*.

In 1750 Diderot fell afoul of the authorities and was thrown into the dungeons at Vincennes for "irreligious writing." Rousseau claimed that he immediately wrote to the king's mistress, Madame de Pompadour, begging her to have Diderot released or let himself be put in prison beside him. A typical histrionic gesture—or boast (no such letter has been found in the archives). What is certain is that Rousseau would walk the six miles out to Vincennes three or four days a week to visit his friend. It was the height of summer, and the excessive heat forced him to walk slowly through the woods. To pass the time he would read the newspaper, and one day he read that the Academy of Dijon was offering a prize. This was for the best essay on the question: "Has the progress of the arts and sciences done more to corrupt or to purify morals?" According to Rousseau, "The moment I read these words, I beheld another universe and became another man." His ensuing reaction, or at least his description of this reaction, is typically over the top: "All at once I felt my mind dazzled by a thousand lights, a crowd of splendid ideas presented themselves to me with such force and in such confusion that I was thrown into a state of indescribable bewilderment. I felt my head seized by a dizziness that resembled intoxication. A violent palpitation constricted me and made my chest heave. Unable to breathe and walk at the same time, I sank down under one of the trees in the avenue and passed the next half hour in such a state of agitation that when I got up I found that the front of my jacket was wet

20

with tears, although I had no memory of shedding any. . . ." Et cetera, et cetera, for lines to come.

Many see this rapture on the road to Vincennes as marking the birth of romanticism. Indeed, it contains in embryo many of the excesses that were to become a central feature of romantic expression. Historically the time was ripe for such indulgent behavior. The Renaissance had seen the initial freeing of the European mind from the stifling constraints and superstitions of medievalism. This liberation had been further advanced by the Enlightenment, with its emphasis on rationalism. But such progress had been achieved at a cost. The Enlightenment marked a largely intellectual advance, and its emphasis on reason tended to suppress the emotions. Civilized behavior was seen as the exercise of restraint—a classic nobility which expressed itself only in "elevated sentiments." This repression of an essential part of human nature would come to an end with the eruption of the romantic movement. Rousseau would in many ways be the man who instigated this movement. His would be the first major attempt to articulate its wants and feelings. His bravery would be to attempt a defense of humanity against the reason that was stifling it. How could he reasonably justify the irrationality that drives us all? How could he show that an essential element of our humanity in fact exists beneath the veneer of civilized reason? With the benefit of modern psychology, it is possible to recognize here an early awareness of the unconscious—and the initial attempt to integrate this destabilizing force into the human personality.

Rousseau would later recall his vision on the road to Vincennes, claiming that what "blazed in my mind for a quarter of an hour under that tree" would shed its light through all his ensuing works. So what exactly did he understand in this moment of truth? Basically, he saw that the answer to the question set by the Academy of Dijon was negative. Progress in the arts and sciences had resulted only in the corruption of humanity.

Rousseau was now thirty-eight years old. The fame and glory he longed for had eluded him. He remained essentially a nobody. This was so different from how he felt within himself, from all that he felt burning in his heart. The essay competition set by the Academy of Dijon was perhaps his last chance, and he decided to enter. What he produced was *A Discourse on the Sciences and the Arts,* into which he poured all his frustrations and disappointments with the way society had treated him. His fundamental thesis was that the history of humanity had been nothing less than a history of calamitous decline. Humanity was essentially good by nature, but it had been corrupted by civilization and culture. This was not due to any inherent seed of corruption, but simply because humanity had taken a wrong turn. He compared the vital simplicity of life in ancient Sparta with the decay of cultured Athens. Ancient Rome too had lost its vitality once it had taken on the habits of civilization. Culture brought only decline: "the arts, letters, and sciences are spread like garlands of flowers around the iron chains by which men are weighed down." Rousseau's first *Discourse* raised a storm of protest in the intellectual circles of Paris—as confined and incestuous then as they are today. He was accused of believing in a golden age which had never existed—except in pastoral poetry and legend. Did he seriously believe that the universities and the theatres should be closed down, that all books should be burned, that culture should be abolished? Were civilized Frenchmen expected to become like peasants? Rousseau also succeeded in the difficult task of uniting both the reactionaries and the progressives—against him. Like Rousseau, a number of conservative Catholic commentators believed that the entire notion of progress was erroneous—the destruction of the medieval world by the Renaissance and the Enlightenment had been a colossal mistake. Yet at the same time they bitterly contested Rousseau's claim that humanity was fundamentally good. On the contrary, Christian teaching showed that humanity was irreparably flawed by original sin. Likewise, Rousseau's attacks on progress and civilization directly contradicted the enlightened beliefs and ideas of his friends *Les Philosophes*.

Diderot had soon been released from prison. Despite Rousseau's reactionary ideas in the *Discourse,* he continued to support his friend, commissioning more articles on music for *L'Encyclopédie.* Rousseau was by now being received in the Paris literary salons. Yet despite his desire for fame, he was no hypocrite. He felt distinctly ill at ease among the fashionable social throng. What he had written in the *Discourse* came from the depths of his being. He was genuinely against society and its corrupting ways—yet here he was being welcomed in its very midst. Overwhelmed, he did his best to conform. Then it was announced that his *Discourse* had won the prize offered by the Academy of Dijon. He was soon being befriended by a number of intellectual aristocratic ladies; and his ideas began to attract a wider attention among the public at large. His *Discourse* had struck a chord in the stagnant French society of the day, and many began to see in it a call to liberty. In high society this was seen more in personal terms, but others began to detect in it political implications. Rousseau too appeared to have found liberty. The gauche unknown scribbler on the brink of middle age was transformed into a celebrity—the "scourge of civilization."

Rousseau reveled in his newfound fame. He was now accepted on his own terms and no longer attempted to ape the public manners of the time. Indeed, he was even expected to be "temperamental." From now on he would reject civilized behavior and simply be himself. As Rousseau later confessed, this course was adopted for more than idealistic reasons. He was temperamentally incapable of being well mannered, and in fact didn't properly understand what this involved. Mme. de Warens might have attempted to teach him the words, but he had no idea of the music.

As regards other music, this definitely was not the case. Rousseau's "enthusiasms" may have made him appear boorish on occasion, but he was not unintellectual and certainly not ignorant. Many were intrigued by his deep knowledge of music. This proved to be more than theoretical. In 1752 he composed an opera called *Le Devin du Village* (The Village Soothsayer). This was quickly recognized as a work of some quality, and a performance was arranged at Fontainebleau in the presence of Louis XV and Madame de Pompadour. The king was so delighted that a day or so later he sent for Rousseau with the intention of awarding him a life pension. But this proved too much.

Rousseau's naked temperament was vulnerable at the best of times. On hearing of the king's invitation he became overwhelmed with shyness. What would he do in the king's presence? What could he say? Then, as ever, he sought justification for his reactions. He began to suspect that his precious "liberty" was under threat. He pretended to be ill, and fled to Paris. Diderot was furious, upbraiding him for his "irresponsibility." He could have been supported for life, but instead he had risked offending the king—no light matter. Fortunately the king did not take umbrage, and the matter was forgotten.

Rousseau now courted further controversy by writing his *Letter on French Music*. As in many autocratic regimes, where freedom of speech is curtailed, music played a central role in the French arts during this period, attracting widespread attention. The music lovers of Paris were now split into two rival factions. *Les Philosophes* and their friends favored the new melodic Italian *opera buffa* (literally "comic opera"), epitomized by the Neapolitan composer Pergolesi, whose work Rousseau had arranged for publication in Paris. The traditionalists,

27

led by the seventy-year-old French composer Rameau, despised these "cheap Italian tunes." They favored the classical restraint of French music, with its emphasis on harmony. The precision and grandeur of such music was seen as an expression of the superiority of French culture. Rousseau's *Letter on French Music* was an early manifesto for romanticism in the arts. It decreed that the creative spirit should give free rein to its expression, untrammeled by the restraints of tradition and formal rules. The new bravura Italian music was infinitely superior to the stick-in-the-mud French style. Rameau and his supporters were outraged at this insult to the glory of France. Rousseau's opinions were deemed seditious, and such was the popular fury that an effigy of Rousseau was hung in public. But Rousseau had his finger on the pulse of the time. Italian music was the style of the future. Ten years later in Vienna, the twelve-year-old Mozart would produce his first opera, *Bastien and Bastienne,* basing it on *Le Devin du Village* and composing the music in "the Italian style."

In 1753 the Academy of Dijon announced another essay prize. This time the question to be addressed was: "What is the origin of equality among men, and is it authorized by Natural Law?" Here "Natural Law" refers to putative universal laws, aligned with the laws of nature, which go beyond the customs, laws, and conventions of any particular society. This would coincide with our modern notion of "basic human rights," except that in Rousseau's time there was a widespread belief that such rights or laws were an integral part of Nature. Remnants of this belief persist in descriptions of human behavior that draw on adjectives such as "unnatural," "inhuman," "evil," and so forth.

For the Academy to pose a question regarding the "origin of equality among men" was highly unusual, considering that this was very much a provincial bourgeois body, which included lawyers, priests, and councillors. Equality was a provocative topic, given the social climate of the period. France was a country under authoritarian rule, whose huge social inequalities were giving rise to the rumblings of an implacable discontent among the downtrodden mass of the population. It was at this time that Madame de Pompadour made her celebrated remark:

29

"*Après nous le déluge*" (After us, it will all be swept away).

On hearing of the new essay competition, Rousseau declared, "If the Academy has the courage to raise the question, I will have the courage to answer it." And he was as good as his word. The result was his first masterpiece, his *Discourse on the Origin of Inequality,* published in 1754. This, more than any other work, has been seen as the intellectual spark that would one day ignite the French Revolution.

In this *Discourse,* Rousseau develops more fully the original idea he had sketched in the first *Discourse.* Natural humanity was originally good; only with the advent of civilization did humanity become corrupt. (Rousseau uses the term "man" rather than humanity. Although both he and the French language are incorrigibly chauvinist in this aspect, I have assumed that here Rousseau is usually referring to all of humanity, rather than a peculiar part of it.) The *Discourse on Inequality* outlines a hypothetical social history of humanity and its fall from natural grace. This time the devil of the piece is seen more as property rather than civilization, culture, and

30

learning. Rousseau points out that humans are the only species that create their own history. This means that we are responsible for our plight (and are thus responsible for getting out of it). When we compare ourselves with other natural creatures, we see that our social corruption has rendered us miserable. We feel unfulfilled, unhappy, and unequal. Yet how has this come about?

As Rousseau saw it, the key to this lay in our inequality—of which there are two types. The first is natural inequality, which comes about through differences in our size, our strength, our intelligence, and such. This inequality is physical and unavoidable. We are neither responsible for it nor can we change it. The second type of inequality arises from society, and does lie within our control. This results from human choice and action. It is both moral and political. Rousseau sketches how this has come about by means of a hypothetical history of humanity. Here Rousseau adopts a "scientific" method to reconstruct the phases through which our social development has passed. This is not actual history, or even actual prehistory, more a primitive early form of psycho-sociology. In this prototypical attempt, Rousseau dispenses with actual evidence in favor of insight on a deeper level. His method may appear hopelessly speculative and "literary" compared to the modern scientific approach, which is more used to having theory backed with solid fact. Yet it is worth bearing in mind that our modern social sciences—which derive from such works—are often forced to a similar resort. Economics, sociology, and even psychology all frequently require belief in a "typical human being"—whose existence has no more factual backing than Rousseau's "man."

Rousseau's conjectural history of the corruption of humanity is intended to reveal the unnaturalness and evil of the second, "artificial" form of human inequality. According to Rousseau, in their earliest stage human beings existed in a solitary state. In this they had "no moral relations or determinate obligations to one another." Under such circumstances, humanity may have lived a somewhat lonely existence, but its individual members were happy and free. Their nature was good.

It is worth comparing this view with the similarly speculative moral fable proposed by the English philosopher Thomas Hobbes a century earlier. According to Hobbes, in its original state of nature the life of humanity before the advent of society was "nasty, brutish, and short." What took place was "a war, of every man against every man." Instead of Natural Law, humanity required a Natural Right—the right to self-preservation. Such a right could be enacted only if human beings surrendered their individual liberty and power to an overall sovereign power, whose rule had to be obeyed by all. According to Hobbes, this alone could create a society that provided humanity with a "peaceable, social, comfortable living."

Rousseau's *Discourse on Inequality* directly opposed this view of society. In the state of nature, individual human beings behaved in a natural way. They were naturally uncorrupted and good. Vice began only when these innocent individuals joined together to form a society. Where Hobbes's fable may be closer to historical fact, Rousseau's has an undeniably psychological force. We lose something of our nature by partaking in society. Even today we can be momentarily aware of a nostalgia for "living in the wild," for "going back to nature." We imagine that by living "closer to nature" we are somehow living closer to our true selves. Even those immune from such rural fantasies would probably concur that domestic social life is in some way "unnatural." A phantasm of Rousseau's ideas lingers on in every New Age rural commune, in the parkland surrounding the banker's mansion, even in the suburban garden.

So what precisely is Rousseau's idea of "natural"? When did we fall from grace? How did "unnatural" society come about? According to Rousseau, this traumatic event occurred when men built the first huts so that they could live together with women. Cohabitation has long been seen as responsible for the fall of man (and women too have their views on this matter). Religion, morality, even psychology can produce strong arguments why these two irreconcilable elements of humanity should be kept apart—indeed, why they should never have come together in the first place. Traditionally this has been seen as the undoing (and indeed the doing) of humanity. But Rousseau's argument goes beyond the unnatural behavior manifested by the domesticated inhabitants of the grass hut, New Age commune, or banker's mansion. We didn't fall from grace, instead we were the victims of a con trick. Society came about as a result of a hoax. "The first man who enclosed a piece of ground, who then came up with the idea of saying 'this is mine' and found people simple enough to believe him . . . was the real founder of evil society." The founding fathers of society were imposters. As Rousseau eloquently warned his readers, "You are lost if you forget that the fruits of the earth belong to everyone and the earth itself belongs to no one!" But the duped victims were not without blame. "All ran headlong to their chains, in hopes of securing their liberty; for they had just wit enough to perceive the advantages of political institutions, without experience enough to enable them to foresee the dangers." There are of course inconsistencies in such a poetic form of argument. If the natural state of humanity was so good, what could human beings possibly perceive as the "advantages of political institutions," and how could these be so great as to prompt them to run "headlong to the chains"?

As with so much of Rousseau—both the man and his ideas—defects in rationality are compensated by perceptive intuitions of human nature. Ignoring his previous argument, he then goes on to claim that in the beginning, "nascent society" was in fact good. Families lived together surrounded by other families, and all lived in harmony. This was humanity's "golden age." But as we learned to love one another, we also became aware of counterbalancing emotions. The ability to admire brought with it the corrupting ability to be jealous. Neighbors began comparing themselves with those around them. This activity "marked the first step toward inequality and at the same time toward vice." The process continued: "Each one began to consider the rest, and to wish to be considered in turn; and thus a value came to be attached to public esteem." People came to require, or demand, respect from those around them. People wanted to be, or be seen to be, better than those around them. In an uncannily prescient passage, Rousseau showed how the current mania for fame is nothing new: "Whoever sang or danced best, whoever was the handsomest, the strongest, the most dexterous, or the most eloquent, came to be of most consideration." Fame—the "value" of "public esteem"—may often appear trivial, but Rousseau shows that it is one of the earliest, or deepest, of our communal assessments and needs. He then takes this a stage further. Along with the family and the wish for social respect, the idea of private property came into being. This turned previous inequalities into a visible reality: some inevitably had more than others. But since property was a reality—a collection of things—it needed physical protection. This gave birth to laws, and a government to enforce these laws. The persistence of government gave rise to formal institutions, which had their own devastating effect. Inequalities became solidified in law, power, and stone. Aspects of natural inequality now became mirrored in their artificial counterparts. Physical weakness had its counterpart in social deference, physical strength was mimicked by social dominance. Rousseau claimed that this "was, or may well have been, the origin of society and law." It may have borne no relation to historical fact, or even to prehistorical sociological truth, but there is no doubting its strength as instructive fairy tale. Just as there is no doubting *how* Rousseau wished us to be instructed. "For the advantage of a few individuals, the whole of humanity was subjected to perpetual labor, to slavery, and to wretched humiliation."

The concept of property was no less than "fatal" to humanity, resulting only in "horrors." This idea would be carried to its logical conclusion in the following century by the French social reformer Georges Sorel, who coined the emotive slogan, "Property is theft." Meanwhile Marx would build communism on similar lines. All property would belong to the state, and in the coming socialist utopia the state would finally "wither away." Leaving what? Presumably Rousseau's Eden, where "the earth itself belongs to no one." Setting aside the sheer impracticality of this dream, there is a crucial difference between Rousseau and Marx here. Where Marx looked forward to an unrealizable future, Rousseau looked back to a past which he realized had never actually existed. Rousseau was writing a parable, Marx was writing a prophecy. Yet there is no denying the powerful influence of Rousseau's ideas on Marx. Rousseau was the man who put "liberty" on the social agenda—and all future revolutions would proclaim this as their goal. On the personal level, this same "liberty" would be central to the whole notion of romanticism. Marx would famously declare: "Philosophers have only *interpreted* the world, what matters is to *change* it." A century beforehand, Rousseau was already putting this into practice.

Rousseau's *Discourse on Inequality* also includes a pungent analysis of society itself. What is the purpose of society? To provide civil peace, and also to protect the property of those who have any. A society thus benefits all individuals who live within it. But it is of most benefit to the rich, as they have the most to be protected. It also introduces a subtle transformation. To begin with, property was simply found and appropriated. The possession of property was in this sense almost accidental. It was a contingent fact. A man simply fenced off some ground and called it his. Society and the rule of law transformed this contingent fact into ownership *by right*. It became a legal possession. The landowner rightfully possessed his land; his neighbor without land was kept dispossessed of it. Both situations were maintained *by law.* In this way society could never be just, because the rich always benefited most, and the law gave them an unfair advantage in keeping them rich. Such injustices inevitably led to envy, fear, and hatred. Only in society did the interests of individuals conflict with one another. This conflict permeated the entire society and had to be masked by the appropriate manners and courtesy. This was why no society was truly happy. Even the rich were not content. The conflicts of society drove them ever onward, so that they too were never satisfied.

Rousseau concluded that inequality was part of the process that separated human beings from their original nature and innocence. In this way humanity became alienated from its real self. "Social man lives constantly outside himself, and only knows how to live in the opinion of others, so that he seems to receive the consciousness of his own existence merely from the judgment of others concerning him." Humanity became set adrift, cut off from its original inner certainty. "Everything is reduced to appearance. Even honor, friendship, virtue, and often vice too, become nothing more than acting and artifice. We are reduced to asking others what we are; we never dare to ask ourselves. . . . All we have to show for ourselves is a frivolous and deceitful appearance, honor devoid of virtue, reason devoid of wisdom, pleasure devoid of happiness." Rousseau's analysis is as recognizable today as it was in pre-Revolutionary France.

So what was the answer? Rousseau in fact provided this at the very outset of his *Discourse,* which was dedicated "To the Republic of Geneva." Beneath this, in his introduction, he characterizes his home city as the ideal state. Here society has succeeded in the impossible: "You have achieved happiness." In their small republic the citizens of Geneva had managed to balance "the equality which nature established among men and the inequality which they have managed to institute amongst themselves." This had been achieved because "you have no masters other than wise laws made by yourselves and administered by upright magistrates of your own choosing."

Quite apart from contradicting the contents

of the ensuing *Discourse*, this paean of praise for his home city was not entirely devoid of the "acting and artifice" that Rousseau so condemned. (Perhaps he couldn't help this, because he was living in an unavoidably "frivolous and deceitful" society like Paris.) Either way, Rousseau had decided that he wanted to return to Geneva, and was unsure of his reception. He had good cause for this. He had renounced his native Calvinism for despised Catholicism, and he had chosen to scandalize public opinion by living openly with a washerwoman who had now produced children. Even a man as insensitive as Rousseau was aware that such things were unlikely to endear him to his puritan fellow citizens. Perhaps some carefully chosen flattery in the introduction to his book might help.

Rousseau had now realized the error of his ways. This had not been easy. His opera had achieved a success when it was performed in Paris, and he now faced the prospect of a successful career as a composer. Fame and money would be his at last. But he would not have this. Perversely true to himself as ever, Rousseau now chose to abandon opera. Such theatre was simply another example of corrupting civilization. He embarked upon a period of austere moral self-reform, deciding it was time for him to re-embrace the strict principles of Calvinism that had permeated his childhood in Geneva. He would return to his native city, cast aside the corruption of Catholicism, and live a proper life amidst a proper society.

All went surprisingly well, and Rousseau was welcomed with open arms by the citizens of Geneva, who were flattered by the return of their famous son. The *Discourse on Inequality* had not won the prize offered by the Academy of Dijon, but it had aroused huge public interest. Rousseau was on the way to becoming the most talked-about figure in France. No longer did it matter that *Les Philosophes* now considered his ideas anathema to their Enlightenment views. Throughout Europe the classical restraint of the Enlightenment was on the verge of giving way to a new unrestrained romanticism. Rousseau would become both the embodiment and the spokesman of this revolution in sensibility.

More surprisingly, the upright citizens of Geneva even managed to tolerate the presence of Rousseau's illiterate mistress Thérèse. Rousseau's self-reform had not gone so far as to include marriage to his washerwoman companion. In Geneva she was simply passed off as a nurse. The fact that this nurse had no children to look after—other than Rousseau himself—was even more scandalous, had the truth been known. For Thérèse had by now given birth to no less than five children. (How many of these were actually Rousseau's has remained a matter of prurient scholarly speculation.) Where were they when Rousseau arrived with their mother in Geneva? We now come to the grimmest unorthodoxy in Rousseau's determinedly unorthodox life. Each of these five children had been delivered shortly after its birth to the Foundlings' Home, down the road from where he lived in Paris. At various times in his life Rousseau would offer various inadequate excuses for this unpalatable fact. These ranged from the intellectual ("Plato maintained that all children should be brought up by the state") to the psychological ("Children don't like the company of old people"—he was now in his forties). The truth is that to be himself, to be true to his difficult nature and fulfill himself as one of the most original thinkers of the eighteenth century, Rousseau was willing to sacrifice everything. Temperament was all. Such self-centeredness, such monstrous egoism, could tolerate the presence of no other child in its life.

Rousseau made little effort to conceal what he had done: he was aware of his guilt, and he suffered from it. As far as his life is concerned, these five children tip the scales very heavily against him. And his writings should not be separated from his life. Indeed, they drew so heavily upon it that such would be impossible. On the other hand, we must ask: does his life fatally compromise his ideas? However grudgingly, I think that in this instance the answer must be "no." Rousseau's ideas would prove to be a major contribution to human self-understanding—on the personal, social, psychological, and philosophical levels. We are all his inheritors, for better or for worse. We can deplore his actions, we can ridicule his irrationalities, but his ideas inform such a wide aspect of our lives that our present existence is inconceivable without them. "Beware the moralist who abandons his children!"—never was a slogan more cause for self-examination.

Rousseau became a citizen of Geneva and was then accepted back into the Calvinist communion, despite reservations in some quarters. Living in Geneva he rediscovered the beauties of nature—marveling at the snow-peaked Alps, rowing across the blue waters of Lake Geneva to the Valois shore, walking up in the foothills to where the waterfalls cascaded through the ravines. Amidst the vast spaces of the mountains, he would lose himself in reverie. "I do not think, I do not reason. I feel myself, with a kind of voluptuousness, possessed of the substance of the universe." But he also had to work, to provide money for himself and Thérèse. Despite his rejection of the corrupting arts, he decided to write a play. Theatre was forbidden in Geneva, and after some months he set out on a visit to Paris. He intended to "set his affairs in order" before returning to live permanently in Geneva.

But it was not to be. Once back in Paris, Rousseau began his round of the salons, where he was flattered to be lionized by society hostesses. He began accepting hospitality at a number of country estates. Finally he decided once more that he was tired of the corruptions of civilization. What he needed was solitude amidst nature—where he could be his natural self, where he could marvel at the simple joys of the natural world and be free to write out his thoughts without interruption. In 1758 he left his meager rooms in Paris to live on the country estate of Madame d'Épinay at Montmorency, in the woods just beyond the northern outskirts of the city. Rousseau was installed at the Hermitage, a restored hunting lodge in a secluded part of the woods, along with Thérèse.

Inevitably there were complications. Madame d'Épinay had a crush on her famous romantic protégé. It had long been recognized that Thérèse was more than simply Rousseau's "nurse," but her coarse appearance and behavior were generally considered to be no threat where his true romantic passions were concerned. Rousseau's relationship with Madame d'Épinay may or may not have remained chaste—it is known that she had another lover during this period—but it is evident that something in Rousseau's multifarious emotional life

remained unfulfilled. Enraptured by his new sur-
roundings, Rousseau embarked upon a novel,
Julie, which was prompted by "a desire for lov-
ing, which I had never been able to satisfy and
by which I felt myself devoured." He claimed
that it expressed his longing for an idealized
love, though the novel itself was deeply concerned with physical love—especially that aspect
of it that appealed to Rousseau's sexuality. The
young male hero, a tutor, is seduced by a beauti-
ful, domineering, aristocratic woman. In an ec-
stacy of passion he declares to her: "Julie, you
were made to rule. Your empire is the most ab-
solute I know . . . your spirit crushes mine. I am
nothing in your presence." One can all but hear
the swish of the cane that first aroused the eight-
year-old boy.

Then one day, while Rousseau was immersed
in writing his novel, a woman "arrived at the
Hermitage wearing boots, piercing the air with
peals of laughter." She had long, wavy black hair
which reached to her waist, was wearing riding
breeches, and was caked up to her knees in mud.
This was Madame Sophie d'Houdentot, a local
aristocratic lady who was in fact Madame

d'Épinay's sister-in-law. She even had the same "full bosoms" as Julie, a feature to which Rousseau draws frequent attention in the novel. Inevitably Rousseau was smitten with love for this dark dominatrix—who quickly "became Julie" in his novel. Rousseau would accompany her on walks in the woods, they would pause beneath a particular acacia tree, and Rousseau would begin reading to her the passionate love letters that the young tutor addressed to Julie in his novel. For her part, Sophie encouraged him, and then at the last moment would upbraid him with "harsh reproaches" for taking liberties—little realizing that this was precisely what Rousseau desired. He was soon driven to a state of "amorous delirium," in which he experienced all the delights of "erotic fervor."

It wasn't long before Madame d'Épinay got wind of this. Although her affair with Rousseau had gone dormant, she was not amused. She wrote to him, "After long showing you every possible mark of friendship and sympathy for several years, there is nothing left for me but to pity you." Rousseau was obliged to leave the Hermitage but was given alternative accommo-

dations by the powerful Maréchel de Luxembourg in a remote cottage on the edge of the
Montmorency woods.

Despite all this emotional turbulence,
Rousseau's four years at Montmorency were to
prove the most creative period of his life. The
most important work of these years was his *Social Contract*. This opens with the ringing declaration: "Man was born free, and everywhere he
is in chains." Liberty is an essential part of our
humanity. "To renounce freedom is to renounce
one's human quality." In his *Discourse on Inequality*, Rousseau had suggested that this was
inevitable when "natural man" came together to
form society. Now he suggests otherwise: there is
a solution to this problem. Human beings are
not corrupted if they form a society by entering
into a genuine social contract. This latter term
presents another historical fiction which is intended as a social parable. When individuals
come together to form a society they must each
contract to surrender something; and in return
the society gives them something back. This is
the hypothetical "social contract." In the *Discourse*, Rousseau shows how individuals surren-

50

der their freedom in return for protection—of their property and other civil rights. Rousseau now insists that it is possible for a genuine social contract to take place between human beings so that they still retain their freedom and thus their humanity. In exchange for their natural freedom, they must be given a *better* freedom—namely, political freedom.

Rousseau introduces himself in the *Social Contract* as a man who has every right to hold forth about justice and the rights of the citizen. He may not be a powerful ruler or a prince with experience in such matters, but he is nonetheless a sovereign. As a citizen of the free state of Geneva, he is its sovereign. His democratic rights make him a ruler of the city. Rousseau is skating on thin ice here. He refers to Geneva a number of times in the *Social Contract,* and in glowing terms. But the Geneva he now refers to is the Geneva established more than two centuries earlier by Calvin. The reality Rousseau had experienced during his return visit in 1754 had evidently proved something of a disappointment. At one point he even goes so far as to describe contemporary Geneva as a dictatorship "run by twenty-five despots." The ideal state of Geneva now had to be viewed through the rosy spectacles of history (a history that Rousseau, and his accompanying "nurse," would have been lucky to survive. During this earlier period, fornication was punished by death).

Despite such historical oversights, Rousseau's analysis is instructive. He goes on to explain how a just society cannot be created by force. In much the same way that physical inequalities are no excuse for social inequalities, imposed rights do not create genuine rights. When force creates rights, those rights are as fleeting as the force itself. As one force deposes another, one set of rights will give way to another. This leads to the state where "might is right." (Those who subscribe to this seductive slogan in order to impose their ideas merely render such ideas ephemeral. The Nazis, who were great believers in "might is right," should thus have seen their total defeat in 1945 as the ultimate disproof of all they had ever stood for.)

In order to establish a proper government, the consent of all the people was required. Only in this way could all its citizens have moral equality. The citizen finds liberty by submitting to the law he has imposed upon himself for the good of all. But there is a difficulty in Rousseau's description of how the just society is put together. The individual is free because he submits only to his own will. In a society there are many wills. Owing to the variety of human nature, these wills inevitably differ and thus conflict. In this event, some individuals are forced to submit to a will that conflicts with their own.

Rousseau attempted to overcome this difficulty by introducing the concept of the "general will." Human society was itself viewed as a collective individual, which retained its collective liberty because it subscribed to its own general will. The general will applied to all because it derived from all. This ensured both liberty and equality as well as fostering a spirit of fraternity. (The "Liberty, Equality, Fraternity" of the modern French Republic's national motto derives directly from these ideas.)

Here Rousseau agreed with Hobbes, who decreed that in the social contract the individual surrenders all his rights to the community. In exchange for laying down his natural rights, the citizen receives civil rights. This benefits all individuals. Outside society, the individual's rights depended upon his individual power. Within society, his rights were enforced by the power of the community: the rule of law. But here we come up against a central difficulty. In Rousseau's words: "If there are opposing voices at the time when the social contract is made, this opposition does not invalidate the contract. It merely excludes these dissidents: they are foreigners among the citizens. After the state is instituted, residence within it implies consent: to live within the state requires submission to the sovereign." If an individual within a society "refuses to obey the general will, he should be constrained to do so." Those who do not submit to the freedom of the sovereign general will "should be forced to be free."

These are ominous words. In the great collective societies of the twentieth century they would take on a clear meaning of their own. Both communism and Nazism excluded their "dissidents" and stigmatized "foreigners among the citizens." Such notions derive directly from Rousseau's *Social Contract*. But their application was disingenuous. Rousseau would certainly not have subscribed to any "dictatorship of the proletariat" (Marx's prescription for how a society would be forced to be free). Nowhere does Rousseau state that an entire society should be forced to be free. He is referring to *individuals* who resist the general will. Even so, this idea still grates with modern notions of liberalism and pluralism.

In the *Social Contract* Rousseau abandons the earlier idea of liberty that he delineated in the *Discourse on Inequality*. Originally, in their natural state, human beings had been free. Now he stresses how natural human beings are not so free at all. They are slaves of their animal passions, and their strength is limited by their natural inequality. Society gives natural human beings a liberty from their enslaving natural passions, as well as a moral equality. Liberty, equality, and fraternity. Although the French lay great claim to rationality, here reason flies out the window. Liberty and equality are in fact incompatible. If people are given liberty, they inevitably develop inequalities. Some work hard to accumulate a fortune, others prefer to seek fulfillment in the pursuit of power or indolence.

Likewise, if people are forced to be equal, their liberty to become unequal must be curtailed. The ideas of freedom and equality such as prevail in a modern liberal democracy are necessarily selective. We are equal before the law; we are at liberty to pursue our different aims. We should have equality of opportunity; but we should be free to follow the opportunity of our choice.

Rousseau too was aware of these difficulties. He may no longer have viewed society as "fatal," but he remained aware of its ability to damage our humanity. Although "the foundation of the social contract is property" and this should be protected, it should not be at all costs. Riches bring power, but "power should never be great enough for its owner to exercise violence." He specifically states that "in respect of riches, no citizen shall ever be wealthy enough to buy another, nor be poor enough to be forced to sell himself." The state should "allow neither rich men nor beggars." He insists: "These two estates, which are naturally inseparable, are equally fatal to the common good; from the one come the friends of tyranny, and from the other tyrants." He realizes that "the force of circumstance tends to destroy equality, [whereas] the force of legislation ought always to tend toward preserving it."

Rousseau distinguished between two types of law. The "actual law," such as is outlined in the *Discourse on Inequality*, simply preserved society as it was, with all its injustices. True law, on the other hand, derived from the will of all the people and ensured justice for all. No intelligent people would ever agree to formulate laws against themselves. But there was a decided problem here. Rousseau found himself forced to concede that most people were not intelligent. The general will might have had the moral backing of the people, but it did not necessarily operate for their own good. People were not always capable of seeing the implications of what they willed.

Rousseau was one of the first liberal thinkers to accept this problem—which remains a persistent difficulty in all enlightened social argument. Even the most liberal commentators are forced to concede that mass behavior must frequently be judged—and legislated for—according to its lowest common denominator. And as fellow participants in this behavior, we all know that this can be very low and very common indeed.

Rousseau's solution was simple. People were better off when they were ruled by a good leader, who was sufficiently skilled to draw up a just constitution and system of laws—so that no mistakes were made. Here Rousseau was ruthlessly pragmatic, even Machiavellian. If necessary, a leader should be willing to suggest that his ideas were the result of divine inspiration—in order to give his rule sufficient force in the public eye.

Rousseau was convinced that a good republican government required the backing of religion. Christianity, however, was no use for such purposes. This religion may have preached brotherly love, but in the main its virtues were directed toward spiritual values. It was concerned with getting people into the next world, the kingdom of heaven, not with telling them how to make a success of their lives in an earthly republic, or even how to make the republic itself a success. Christianity was worse than useless here. What was needed was a civil religion which encouraged civil virtues such as courage and patriotism. Such virtues brought success to the citizen and at the same time brought benefit to the state.

Here Rousseau was articulating a growing European realization—though one that remained necessarily covert, as it directly contravened Christian orthodoxy and the teaching of the church. The ideas upon which Rousseau drew in this instance had been set down most explicitly by the Dutch thinker Bernard Mandeville, who in 1714 had written *The Fable of the Bees*. In this Mandeville pointed out that the virtues required by public life were precisely the opposite of the private behavior required by Christianity. What Christianity condemned as vices were the very virtues that drove civil life: greed, self-interest, ambition, and vanity. As Mandeville put it: "private Vices are public Benefits." While Rousseau didn't go quite as far as this, he still saw the need for a civil religion. This would contain a minimal religious element while encouraging political and martial virtues. Once again, hindsight enables us to see the seeds of fascism here. A devious leader at the head of a civil religion—such a situation was fraught with danger.

The *Social Contract* was published in 1762 and met with a decidedly mixed reaction. Many saw in it the way to future liberty and a just society. Others were less impressed. The citizens of Geneva had not expected such ingratitude. The authorities ("the twenty-five despots") ordered the book to be burned. Worse than the insult to their city was the willful misrepresentation of their religion. Here they had a point. Their Calvinism was both genuinely Christian and genuinely patriotic. Geneva had been required to fight for its religious freedom. Indeed, the separation of religion and civic virtue is not quite as clear as Rousseau (or Mandeville) suggest. In the following century the Greek Orthodox church would be largely responsible for uniting the Greeks in their patriotic struggle for freedom from the Ottoman Turks. Similarly, in the twentieth century the Roman Catholic church played an integral role in maintaining Polish resistance against their Communist oppressors. In such cases the coming together of politics and religion

60

was a civic benefit. But such effective union is temporary. Only civic religion seeks a permanent union: the Nazi "thousand-year reich," the Communist march toward the inevitable "withering away of the state," and similar delusions. In the long run, civic religion invariably proves detrimental to both spiritual values and civic ones. Religious belief and political belief share only the fact that they are both faiths.

Meanwhile Rousseau had won the hearts of many with the publication of his novel *Julie, or The New Hélöise*. The passionate antics of the tutor-hero Saint-Preux, whose resemblance to Rousseau even extends to his age, caught the public imagination. All the world loves a lover. Saint-Preux may have been forty-nine, but like his creator he remained a teenager at heart. His seduction of his young pupil (or vice versa) was appreciated for its overheated emotional intensity rather than any relation to reality. Rousseau never in fact became Sophie's lover. Likewise, a middle-aged tutor who seduces his young aristocratic charge and makes her pregnant (as Saint-Preux did Julie) is liable to end up in court, then as now. Not for nothing has Saint-Preux been seen as the predecessor of Humbert Humbert in *Lolita.*

Nonetheless, the appeal of *Julie* was universal. Here was a description of emotional rapture in an actual setting—the countryside along the shores of Lake Geneva. Despite its ecstasies over the beauty of nature and the joys of love, this was no legendary romance, no pastoral idyll populated by gods and mythical figures. These were real people living domestic lives—people with whom the reader (and the writer) could identify. And Rousseau's readers responded every bit as enthusiastically as he did. Here was one of the inaugurating works of romanticism.

It is difficult to exaggerate the full import of early romanticism in Europe. Hero worship, popular idols, emotional identification, role models—all these are now an understood element of modern society. In the mid-eighteenth century the only heroes and idols available were saints or legendary figures—far removed from everyday experience. Respect and awe were concentrated upon the equally distant figures of rulers—local lords or far-off royalty. And all such veneration was restrained by social and religious norms. Meanwhile civilized behavior was judged in cultural terms. Civilized emotion—tellingly defused as "sentiment"—was similarly elevated and rational. The Enlightenment had inspired widespread intellectual advances—and equally widespread emotional repression. The emotional self-confidence of Renaissance humanism had been superseded by the uncertainties of the intellectual search for certainty and the advance of rigorous science. Philosophers now sought to define the emotions rather than liberate them or learn how to live with them. Rousseau's novel addressed a pent-up need, especially among the new breed of educated women. In *Julie*, Rousseau's expression of emotion is intense and incoherent. This is both its strength and its validity. He did not fully understand himself what he was expressing, but he knew its truth within him. His troubled soul refused to submit to rational restraints.

The fire that Rousseau lit would soon become a conflagration. To name the successors to *Julie* is to record the landmarks of a newly illuminated region in human self-expression. In the following decade Goethe would write his early

Sturm und Drang ("storm and stress") master-piece *The Sorrows of Young Werther.* In music the classical lyricism of Mozart would soon give way to the turbulent emotionalism of Beethoven's *Moonlight Sonata* and the *Eroica ("Heroic") Symphony.* Later Byron would epitomize himself as the "gloomy egoist" in his auto-biographical *Childe Harold's Pilgrimage.* Young women were far from being the only ones affected by this resurgence of deep emotion. The fictional suicide of Goethe's *Werther* would inspire a rash of suicides among sensitive young German students. Both men and women fainted during performances of Beethoven. And a generation of European poets, from Pushkin to Leopardi, would idolize Byron.

Rousseau followed *Julie, or The New Hélöise* with another work in the guise of fiction entitled *Émile, or On Education.* This is in part a novel describing how a rich man's son is educated by his tutor. The narrative is interrupted by long digressions on how this education ought to be conducted, together with philosophical reflections on the very nature of our humanity. The book contains a curious mixture of the romanticism of

Julie and the republicanism of the *Social Contract*. Where the latter aimed at social liberty, *Émile* is more concerned with personal liberty and how it enables us to achieve fulfillment, happiness, and wisdom. This is also seen as a suitable education for the young citizens of the ideal republic described in the *Social Contract*.

Rousseau's attitude toward children marks a watershed in our understanding of this difficult subdivision of humanity. Rousseau's ideas are the foundation of our own ideas on children. In the eighteenth century his ideas were considered revolutionary. Before then, children were usually treated as if they were ignorant and unruly miniature adults. During their immaturity they would simply be dispatched into the hands of a servant or nurse. This person was frequently a peasant, who would herself be regarded as a kind of coarse, overgrown child. In the presence of genuine adults, the dwarfish adult was expected to ape the manners of his or her seniors. "Childish" behavior (such as Rousseau knew all too well) was simply unacceptable. There was little or no understanding of what it meant to be a child. This may seem a curious blind spot, considering that all adults had inevitably undergone this experience. But the fact is they had not: for the most part children had simply not been allowed to be children. Instead they had been apprentice adults. Tellingly, the saying "Boys will be boys" did not come into use until well into the nineteenth century.

In *Émile*, Rousseau often shows considerable psychological insight into the behavior of children. He describes how during infancy when a child cries we try to silence it, either by giving in to its demands or by threatening it. "Thus his first ideas are those of domination and servitude. Before knowing how to speak, he commands; before being able to act, he obeys." The initial aim of education should be to replace the child's dependence upon adults with a healthy sense of its own independence. Instead of simply conforming to the wishes and ambitions imposed upon it by adults, the child should be allowed to cultivate its own faculties in accordance with its own development. As Rousseau puts it, "Nature wants children to pass through childhood before becoming men." (As can be seen from the preceding quote, Rousseau's children are male. This was not for the most part his intention in *Émile*. In the attempt to include both sexes, I have perhaps perversely rendered the children sexless. Women reading this text may be encouraged by this procedure; children may have other views.)

According to Rousseau, to begin with children exist in a state of nature. This is analogous, though not identical, to the state of nature in which humanity existed before it became civilized, as described in Rousseau's first *Discourse*. In this early stage the child has no conception of good and evil. These are imposed upon it by outside forces. In *Émile*, Rousseau shows how the tutor should do his best to oppose such forces. His aim should be to encourage the child's nature rather than thwart it. Here Rousseau distinguishes between forms of education. The education of the natural human being, who lives for himself alone, should be balanced with the education of the civil human being, whose life is directed toward the community. This latter form of education inevitably restricts the natural humanity of the child, transforming it into a communal nature. The child's independent identity is reduced to a relative identity within society.

67

Only when these different forms of education are successfully combined are the contradictions in our humanity overcome and happiness achieved. As Rousseau explains elsewhere, "Let us start by becoming what we are, by focusing our attention solely upon ourselves." We should try to discover our true selves, isolating our genuine nature from alien elements which are simply imposed upon it. For only by being ourselves will we ever achieve true knowledge of humanity—and thus be able to enter into the community without losing ourselves.

Rousseau admitted that the tutor's task here is not easy. In helping his pupil discover the truth of his own nature, he need not always be truthful himself. As in the larger social sphere, once again Rousseau encourages Machiavellian methods. If deviousness or even plain deceit are necessary to achieve his aim, the tutor must employ such tactics. On the other hand, he should under no circumstances ever resort to corporal punishment. Brainwashing is evidently preferable to beating. (This has a recognizable parallel with the community where individuals are "forced to be free.")

As in the *Social Contract,* Rousseau has his own unorthodox ideas about religion—both the part it should play and what kind of religion it should be. Where education is concerned, instead of a civil religion the pupil should be taught a personal religion. Rousseau explains this religion at some length and with typical fervor. This is very much his own version of Christianity. Despite his unorthodoxies, Rousseau would always remain a man of deep religious feeling. Yet his rejection of religious dogma and the teachings of the church were equally heartfelt. His articles of faith were simple. He believed in God's love of humanity and in the immortality of the soul. Beyond all rational dictates or religious authority was the "divine voice of the soul in man." With consistent inconsistency, he even goes so far as to back this simple faith with rational argument. Ultimately "all physical and bodily motion [in] the world is commanded by a wise and powerful will." This is God. And how does he know this? "I see it; or rather I feel it." The design of the world indicates the lovingkindness of the being who created it. Elsewhere Rousseau would back this argument with more personal psychological reasons which would seem, in his case, to run closer to the truth: "I have suffered too much to live without faith."

Rousseau covers a wide range of topics in *Émile*. Many of the ideas in this work are as original as its author. In so many ways his vision of humanity was far ahead of its time. Yet curiously, despite the leading role they had played in his life, he had little of originality to say about women. For once, his views were very much of their time: "the proper purpose of women is to produce children." He goes on to claim: "What are failings for men, are women's good qualities." The self-centeredness behind such views soon becomes apparent: "Women ought to direct their knowledge to the study of men and the understanding of taste." The context of this remark makes it clear that the aim of the former study was not scientific—in order to gain knowledge of an apparently alien species, for instance. This study was intended to enable women to support men better. On the other hand, the placing of men and taste in different categories was perhaps not entirely intentional.

When *Émile* was published in 1762 it caused

a sensation. The Archbishop of Paris was not the only one to be outraged by Rousseau's views on religion. The Parlement went so far as to order the public executioner to burn the book publicly, along with the immediate arrest of its author. Even Rousseau's powerful protector, the Marechal de Luxembourg, was unable to defend him from the wrath of the authorities. All he could do was provide Rousseau with a fast carriage to flee the country. Sophie, Madame de Luxembourg, and several other of his female "well-wishers" lined up to bid him a tearful farewell, and he sped off in the nick of time. In the best traditions of French farce, Rousseau's speeding carriage even passed the carriage containing the officers sent to arrest him, speeding in the opposite direction.

Rousseau fled to Switzerland, wisely choosing to make for the canton of Bern rather than his native Geneva—where renewed book burnings had already begun. But he was soon obliged to leave Bern, just ahead of another banning order. For the rest of his life he would remain a fugitive, his oversensitive character degenerating ever deeper into paranoia in the process. Eventually he managed to reach England, where he was befriended by the Scottish philosopher Hume. But by now Rousseau was all but certifiably insane. Dressed theatrically in "Armenian costume," his moods were liable to swing from ecstasy to tears, his paranoia constantly goaded by the vindictive Thérèse, whom he saw as the only person never to betray him. His passionate embraces for Hume in the evening would be followed by vituperative letters in the morning. After seventeen months of emotional mayhem, Rousseau decided to return secretly to France. Dressed incognito in his trademark Armenian costume, he stepped ashore at Calais. Fortunately he was soon given refuge by powerful aristocratic protectors. He would end up staying in semi-secrecy at a cottage on the estate of the Marquis de Girardin at Ermenonville.

Incredibly, given his mental state, it was during this period that Rousseau produced what many regard as his finest work, his *Confessions*. This is literature rather than philosophy, though it contains much penetrating psychological speculation on a subject Rousseau considered to be of deep philosophical importance—himself. He declares: "I would like to be somehow able to make my heart . . . transparent as crystal so that it cannot hide any of its movements." He is as good as his word, and the result is a switchback of emotion—from the immensely moving to the farcical. Yet he knows what he is doing, and his insights into himself cannot help but strike a chord in the reader. Even his attempts to justify the unjustifiable make heartrending reading. He ends with the challenging declaration: "Whoever . . . will examine my nature, my character, my morals, my likings, my pleasures, and my habits with his own eyes and will be able to believe me a dishonorable man, should himself be throttled." Both the naked honesty of this remark, and the violence, would bear fruit.

Despite everything, there were still moments of peace. Rousseau was now more convinced than ever that Thérèse was the only person who had never betrayed him. At the age of fifty-six he finally married her. This took place at a curious ceremony conducted by himself, during which all present burst into tears. Thérèse responded by later falling in love with the Marquis de Girardin's English valet.

73

In between writing, Rousseau would row on a nearby lake. Here he felt "out of reach of my wicked persecutors." Once again he found solace in nature. "Often leaving my boat to the mercy of wind and water, I abandoned myself to reveries. . . . Sometimes I cried out with emotion, 'O nature, O my mother, here I am under your sole protection.'" On July 1, 1778, he collapsed. Next day, as he lay in bed, he addressed the blue sky through his open window. "The gate is open and God awaits me." He tried to get up, fell forward, and died in the arms of Thérèse. He was sixty-six.

Eleven years later the French Revolution would put an end to the *ancien régime,* ushering in the France of "Liberty, Equality, Fraternity." For better or worse, Rousseau's ideas had entered the public domain. Here they would play their part in inspiring the best and the worst of political developments during the ensuing two centuries. From the joyful liberty of the early days of the Revolution to the days when so many were "forced to be free" during the Terror; through romanticism and nineteenth-century social utopianism; through twentieth-century communism, with its ideals and its horrors; through fascism; to the social revolution of the sixties—all these would contain ingredients of Rousseau's ideas. Such was the power of his thought that it could not simply be dismissed by pointing out its inconsistencies. Such were its ecstatic gestures, its liberty, its irrationalities, and its unconsidered consequences that it was perhaps bound to provoke excess. Yet much of this very same thought has quietly settled to become the bedrock of our modern belief about ourselves, as well as our instinctive expectations of a just society.

From Rousseau's Writings

Consider, by contrast, the morals of the few nations who have been preserved from the contagion of useless knowledge. By their virtues they have become happy in themselves and provide a shining example to all. Thus were the first inhabitants of Persia, a nation so exceptional that its inhabitants were taught virtue in the same way as we are taught the sciences. These were the Persians who conquered Asia with ease, and achieved the rare glory of having the history of their political institutions read by posterity as a philosophical romance. So also were the Scythians, of whom history speaks so highly. So also were the early Germanic people, whose simplicity of living, innocence, and virtue were such a delight to the historian Tacitus, when he became sick of describing the crimes and degeneracies of his own enlightened, opulent, and voluptuous people. So also were the Romans themselves in the early days of their poverty and ignorance.

—*Discourse on the Sciences and the Arts*

The first man who enclosed a piece of land, who then came up with the idea of saying "this is mine" and found people simple enough to believe him, was the true founder of civil society. How many crimes, wars, and murders stem from this act. How much misery and horror the human race would have been spared if someone had simply pulled out the stakes and filled in the ditch and cried out to his fellow men: "Beware of listening to this imposter. You are lost if you forget that the fruits of the earth belong to everyone and that the earth itself belongs to no one!"

—*Discourse on the Origin of Inequality*

Man was born free, and everywhere he is in chains. Many a person believes himself to be the master of others, and yet he is in reality a greater slave than they are. How has this change come about? I do not know. What can render it legitimate? I believe that I have the answer to this question.

If I considered only the use of force and its results, I should say that for as long as people are forced to obey and do obey, it works fairly well. But as soon as these people are able to shake off their yoke, and do so by force, things become better. For if people recover their freedom in the same way as it was taken away from them, either they are justified in so gaining their freedom, or there was no justification for taking away their freedom in the first place.

—*Social Contract*

Everything is good in so far as it is given to us by the hands of the Author of Nature. Yet everything degenerates in the hands of man. He forces one country to nurture what is produced in another; one tree to bear the fruits of another. He mixes up and confuses the climates, the elements, and even the seasons. He mutilates his dog, his horse, and his slave. He turns everything upside down, and disfigures everything. He loves deformity and monsters. He will have nothing as Nature made it, not even himself. Like a wild horse, he must be first broken in before he is fit for man's service—he must be shaped according to his own fancy, like a tree in his garden.

—*Émile, or On Education*

I am made quite unlike anyone I have ever met. I will even go so far as to say that I am quite unlike anyone else in the whole world. I may be no better than anyone else, but at least I am different. Whether Nature was right or wrong to break the mold after creating me is a question which can only be resolved after you have read this book.

—*Confessions*

Thus my third child was taken to the Foundling Hospital, just like the other two. The next two were disposed of in the same way, for I had five altogether. This arrangement seemed to me so admirable, so rational, and so legitimate, that the only reason I did not boast openly of it was to spare the mother [Thérèse]. I certainly told all those among my friends who knew of our relationship. . . . In other words, I made no mystery of what I did. This was not only because I have never known how to keep a secret from my friends, but also because I really saw no harm in it. All things considered, what I chose for my children was for the best for them, or so I genuinely believed. I could have wished, and still wish, that I had been reared and brought up in the same fashion.

—*Confessions*

Chronology of Significant Philosophical Dates

6th C B.C.	The beginning of Western philosophy with Thales of Miletus.
End of 6th C B.C.	Death of Pythagoras.
399 B.C.	Socrates sentenced to death in Athens.
c 387 B.C.	Plato founds the Academy in Athens, the first university.
335 B.C.	Aristotle founds the Lyceum in Athens, a rival school to the Academy.

324 A.D.	Emperor Constantine moves capital of Roman Empire to Byzantium.
400 A.D.	St. Augustine writes his *Confessions*. Philosophy absorbed into Christian theology.
410 A.D.	Sack of Rome by Visigoths heralds opening of Dark Ages.
529 A.D.	Closure of Academy in Athens by Emperor Justinian marks end of Hellenic thought.
Mid-13th C	Thomas Aquinas writes his commentaries on Aristotle. Era of Scholasticism.
1453	Fall of Byzantium to Turks, end of Byzantine Empire.
1492	Columbus reaches America. Renaissance in Florence and revival of interest in Greek learning.
1543	Copernicus publishes *On the Revolution of the Celestial Orbs*, proving mathematically that the earth revolves around the sun.

1633	Galileo forced by church to recant heliocentric theory of the universe.
1641	Descartes publishes his *Meditations*, the start of modern philosophy.
1677	Death of Spinoza allows publication of his *Ethics*.
1687	Newton publishes *Principia*, introducing concept of gravity.
1689	Locke publishes *Essay Concerning Human Understanding*. Start of empiricism.
1710	Berkeley publishes *Principles of Human Knowledge*, advancing empiricism to new extremes.
1716	Death of Leibniz.
1739–1740	Hume publishes *Treatise of Human Nature*, taking empiricism to its logical limits.
1781	Kant, awakened from his "dogmatic slumbers" by Hume, publishes *Critique of Pure Reason*.

Great era of German metaphysics begins.

1807   Hegel publishes *The Phenomenology of Mind*, high point of German metaphysics.

1818   Schopenhauer publishes *The World as Will and Representation*, introducing Indian philosophy into German metaphysics.

1889   Nietzsche, having declared "God is dead," succumbs to madness in Turin.

1921   Wittgenstein publishes *Tractatus Logico-Philosophicus*, claiming the "final solution" to the problems of philosophy.

1920s   Vienna Circle propounds Logical Positivism.

1927   Heidegger publishes *Being and Time*, heralding split between analytical and Continental philosophy.

1943   Sartre publishes *Being and Nothingness*, advancing

84

Heidegger's thought and instigating existentialism.

1953   Posthumous publication of Wittgenstein's *Philosophical Investigations*. High era of linguistic analysis.

Chronology of Rousseau's Life and Times

1712	June 28, Jean-Jacques Rousseau born in Geneva, Switzerland.
1727	Death of Newton.
1728	Teenage Rousseau flees from Geneva.
1731	Stays with Madame de Warens and converts to Roman Catholicism.
1742	Arrives in Paris.
1743–1744	Secretary to French ambassador in Venice.

1744	Forms relationship with Thérèse Levasseur.
1750	Writes *Discourse on the Sciences and the Arts*.
1751	Composes opera *Le Devin du Village*.
1755	Publishes *Discourse on the Origin of Inequality*.
1758	Leaves Paris to live at Montmorency.
1761	Publication of *Julie, or The New Hélöise*.
1762	Publication of *Social Contract* and *Émile, or On Education*. Forced to flee to Switzerland.
1766–1767	Takes refuge in England.
1767	Returns to France incognito.
1768	Marries Thérèse Levasseur.
1776	American Independence.
1777	July 2, death at Ermenonville.
1782–1789	Publication of *Confessions*.
1789	French Revolution.

Recommended Reading

Isaiah Berlin, *Against the Current: Essays in the History of Ideas* (Princeton University Press, 2001). This selection of essays contains "The Counter-Enlightenment," which places Rousseau in the philosophical context of his time.

Maurice Cranston, *Jean-Jacques: The Early Life of Jean-Jacques Rousseau, 1712–1754* (University of Chicago Press, 1991). The first volume of the finest and most readable of the many long biographies of Rousseau.

Maurice Cranston, *The Noble Savage: Jean-Jacques Rousseau, 1754–1762* (University of Chicago Press, 1999). The second volume of Cranston's masterwork, taking his subject through the years of the *Social Contract*.

Jean-Jacques Rousseau, *Confessions,* translated by J. M. Cohen (Penguin, 1953). The famous autobiography, which reads like a novel. Its tone reveals the man, even if its content does not always quite reveal the truth.

The Essential Rousseau, edited and translated by Lowell Blair (New American Library, 1991). Selections from Rousseau's major works, as well as a good range of his ideas on social, artistic, political, and philosophical themes.

Robert Wokler, *Rousseau* (Oxford University Press, 1995). An excellent introduction to many aspects of Rousseau's life, including a succinct summary of the ideas in his major works.

Index

A NOTE ON THE AUTHOR

Paul Strathern has lectured in philosophy and mathematics and now lives and writes in London. A Somerset Maugham prize winner, he is also the author of books on history and travel as well as five novels. His articles have appeared in a great many publications, including the *Observer* (London) and the *Irish Times*. His own degree in philosophy was earned at Trinity College, Dublin.